COMIC COMPANION

Unless otherwise indicated, any and all Scripture quotations or references contained in the Cross Man Comics are taken from the Holy Bible, King James version. All Rights Reserved.

LessonsForLifeBooks.com

IMPRINT A Cross Man Comics Supplemental Edition

Comic
Companion

© 2016 by
Keith M. Hammond
is published by
Lessons for Life Books, Inc.
St. Paul, MN 55116

No part of this book may be reproduced or utilized in any for or by any means, electronic or mechanical, including photocopying, recording, or by any information storage or retrieval system, without permission in writing from the Publisher.

Inquiries should be addressed in writing by email to:
permissionrequest@LessonsForLifeBooks.com

ISBN 13: 978-1938588815. Printed in the U.S.A.

Cover design and layout by Keith M. Hammond.
Story concept and 3D Illustrations by Keith M. Hammond.
NOTE: Several software applications and 3D models and 3D props were used to create and generate and render the scenes and characters contained within this and other Cross Man Comics adventures. All are used by purchase or permission.

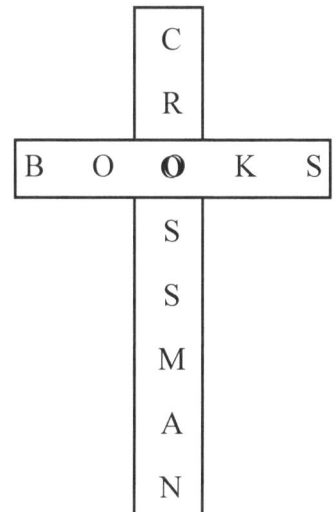

```
        C
        R
B O O K S
        S
        S
        M
        A
        N
```

COMIC SERIES
$12.99 EA.

3 books in this series
Released Sept/Oct 2016

Look Inside on Amazon and
Preview Pages via the Publisher.

FULL COLOR - 3D ILLUSTRATED
An epic and exciting adventure featuring Cross Man and his team of stronghold destroyers as they battle the Devil and his den of darkness, dungeons, demons, dogs, and dragons.

DEMONS IN THE DARKNESS

COMING SOON...An animated film based on this series!

58 Pgs Paperback
9781938588983
$12.99

56 Pgs Paperback
9781938588976
$12.99

58 Pgs Paperback
9781938588815
$12.99

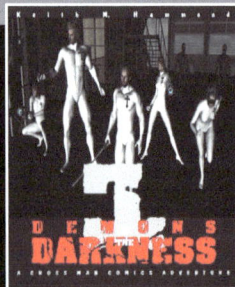

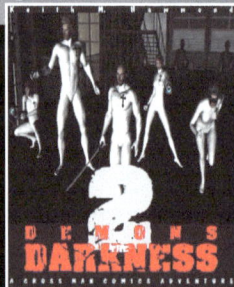

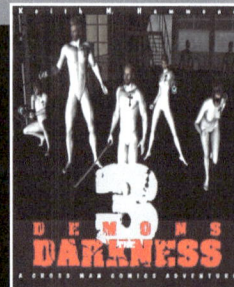

Table of Contents

Copyright 2016 Keith M. Hammond
All Rights Reserved.

Based on the 3 books in the Demons in the Darkness comic series, welcome to 60 pages full of pictures, inside information, names, places, powers and more!

Go behind the story with the author, writer, producer and director of the soon to be released animated film!

+ Find out how the story came about.
+ See it all take place from screen shots of the animation.
+ Get links to inside footage of the movie being made.

See behind the scenes interviews as they are released!

Get and stay connected to the books and the film and come along with us as this amazing adventure gets underway right before our eyes!

In this Comic Companion, you'll:

+ See the Characters.
+ Learn their names, ranks and stories.
+ Read about their powers and weapons.
+ Discover their strengths and weaknesses.
+ Find out more about the series and film.
+ Get links to video clips of them in action!

I appreciate your interest and certainly welcome your input with much grace and gratitude.

Humbly,

Keith M. Hammond

Keith M. Hammond

ABOUT THE AUTHOR

Keith M. Hammond

+ 32 years marriage
+ 2 adult daughters both married
+ 4 grandchildren
+ 20 years in church leadership
+ Wife retired after 20 year nonprofit career
+ Many degrees and certifications
+ Designed and built a high school in 2000
+ Designs churches/schools for other pastors
+ Writes software programs and databases
+ Producing a feature film and TV pilot
+ Opened Books 'N Tea cafe` in 2013
+ Owns Lessons For Life Books

Keith M. Hammond is the author of dozens of books. His passion and purpose to serve The Lord is the foundation for his life, mission and ministry.

He has dozens of video messages and podcasts. The author has lived in Minnesota 25 years, and has interviewed, written articles about, and filmed many celebrities. He is a valued asset to the Body of Christ, and remains humble and helpful to those needing support on their journey.

A catalog of 30 of his most recent books is at:
LessonsForLifeBooks.com/catalog

More about the author at PastorKeith.org

More pics at PastorKeith.org/pkfamily

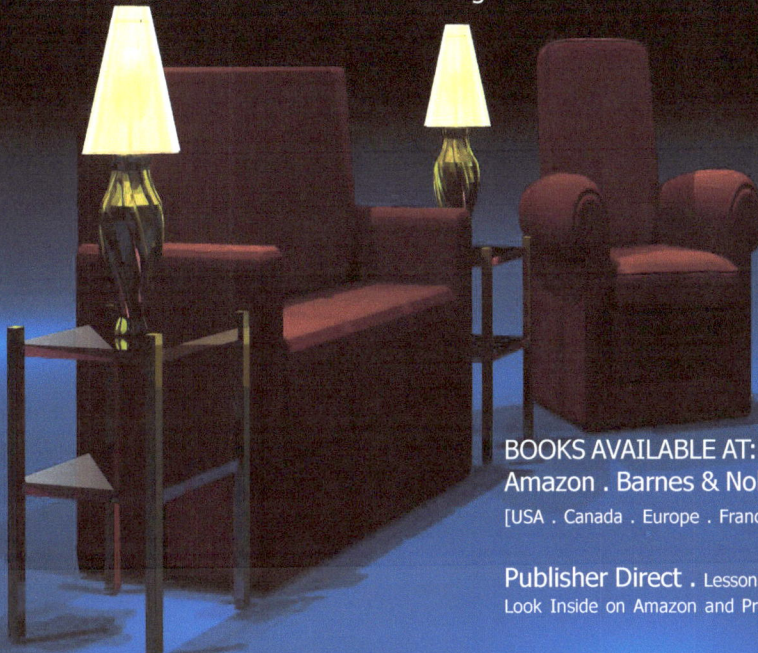

BOOKS AVAILABLE AT:
Amazon . Barnes & Noble . Bookwire.com
[USA . Canada . Europe . France . India . China . and more]

Publisher Direct . LessonsForLifeBooks.com
Look Inside on Amazon and Preview Pages via the Publisher.

When I first began this series I knew what I wanted to accomplish, but I had no idea where to begin to make it happen. Although I had written and published four other 3D full color illustrated series prior to this one, the concept and course of this one, was much different.

As I set out to select a pipeline for the work to be done, I knew it would be vastly different from the software and platform I use for my other series. My plans were to turn this series into an animated film, so the 3D programs I use for the other series would not work for this one.

As I began this journey, it became clear that I was on the right path when the work began to flow without any obstacles. Typically, when I'm preparing to write a book, or actually writing a book, there is a checklist that I go through before and during the process. When those things started falling into place, I knew this project was going to be OK.

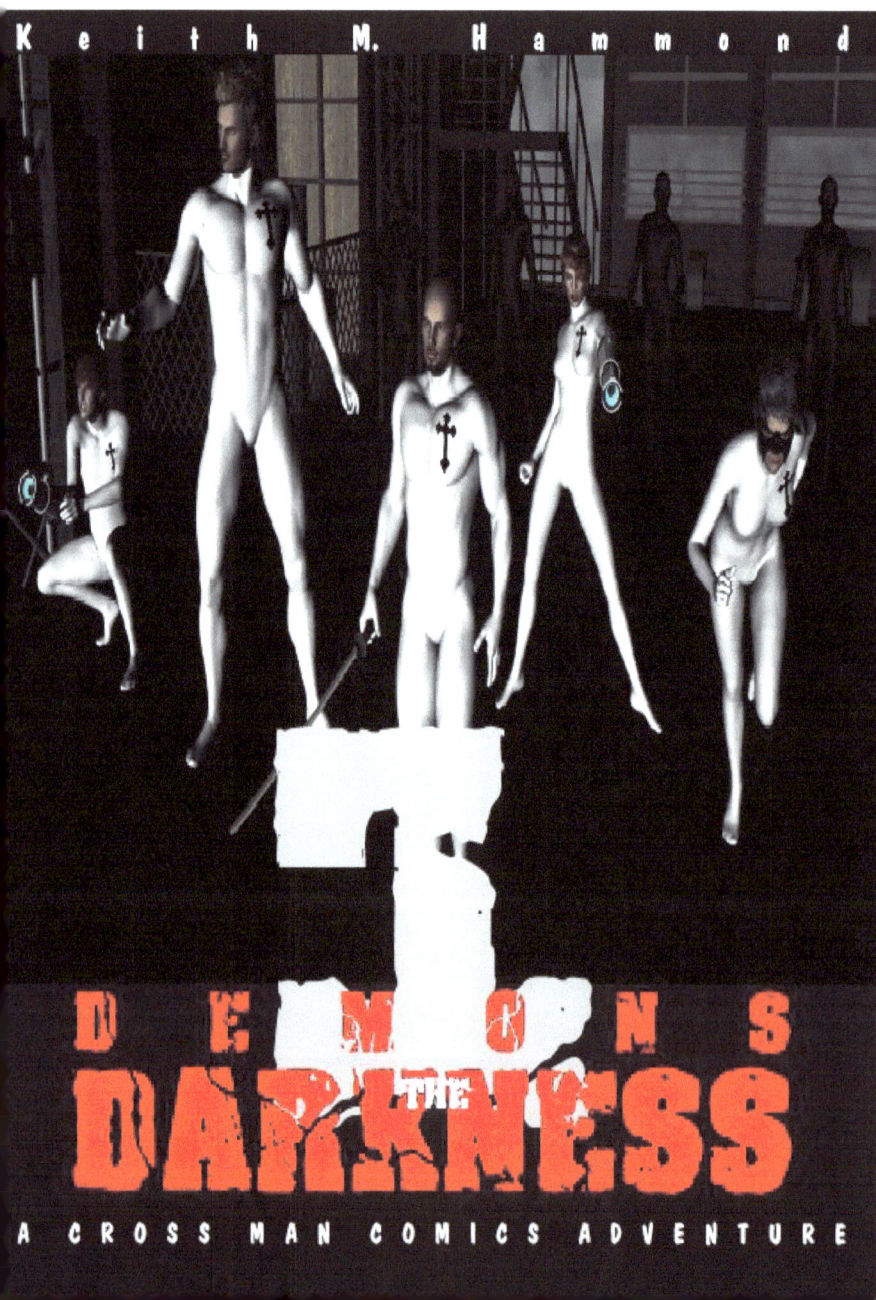

PREMISE

Book One begins Cross Man's quest. It takes place post rapture when Satan is on the Earth being allowed to wreak havoc in the lives of people.

Cross Man and his team are all former members of elite units who were once deployed to help defend the nation from our enemies, who now have all volunteered to remain on the planet to help those who are left behind.

Satan's plans are to steal, kill, and destroy any and everything that gives people any type of hope or help.

If he steals all the food, kills what's left of the light, and destroys the water, he'll have control of the people and the city.

Captain Cross and his team are dedicated and determined to stop the Devil at all cost.

And they know it will not be easy.

58 Pgs Paperback
ISBN 9781938588983 $12.99
Released August 2016

Available at most major retailers and at LessonsForLifeBooks.com

Defending people against an enemy they can sometimes see and at other times cannot see is difficult. Even in our own lives when there are people who are intent upon doing us harm sitting worlds away from us using their own devices to devise ways of damaging us and our endeavors, it's difficult to determine who and how.

I wanted to bring some of that reality into book two. Book one ends with Captain Cross fighting against a mega-dragon inside the Devil's Dark Lair. The battle continues in book two but quickly moves into another part of the story where the Devil has devised another way to distract, destruct and destroy.

As I began to lay out the storyboard for this book the scenes and dialog fell into place. It's not always cut and dry. There are some situations where I've ended up writing an entire story, then trashed it because it just didn't work on the pages when it was produced. I guess if it was easy everyone would be doing it, and I've learned a lot of very valuable lessons through trial and error.

PREMISE

Book Two begins where book one ends. Captain Cross is in the Devil's Den battling against the mega-dragon when he is called to the surface.

Satan has set up an intake center for people to come and sell their souls. As amazing as that sounds the concept of it as it flowed onto the pages made me realize that it's not much different than how he sets up shop in reality.

In this book, Satan has placed a force field around the facility and is only allowing soul-sellers to penetrate it.

Captain Cross and his team have to find a way to not only get pass the barrier, but stop people from willingly walking inside.

After much effort from each member of the team they realize that its not going to be as easy as it seems.

Much more action is underway.

56 Pgs Paperback
ISBN 9781938588976 $12.99
Released September 2016

Look inside on Amazon and Preview Pages at LessonsForLifeBooks.com

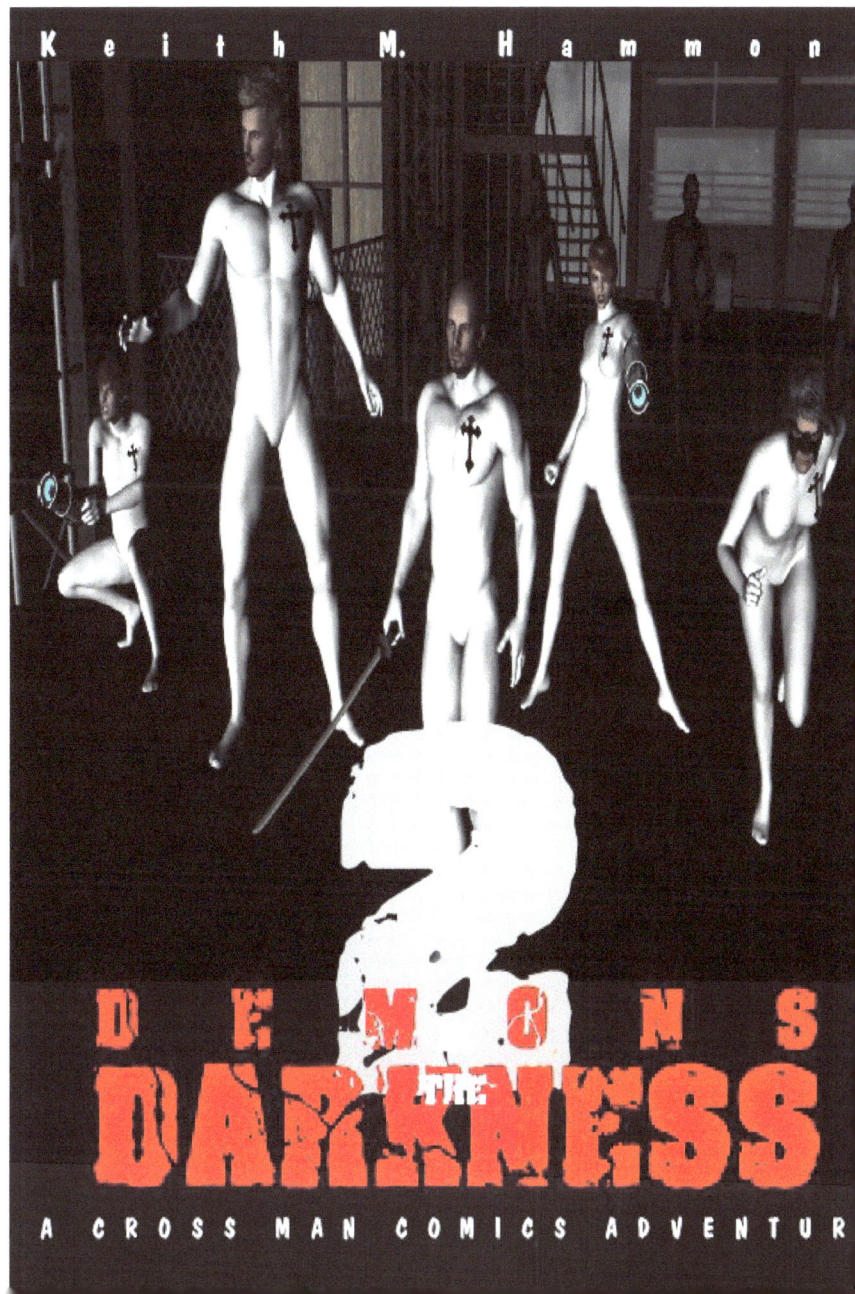

Keith M. Hammon

2

DEMONS
THE
DARKNESS

A CROSS MAN COMICS ADVENTUR

Before I began work on book three I started the process of animating some of the scenes from books one and two, in order to created a trailer to promote the film. When the scenes began to render with ease using the pipeline and workflow I had decided upon, I knew something great was going to come from this.

Projects come and go. Sometimes they work, other times they don't. Some books sell, some don't. But this process taught me procedure on top of the plethora of patience and tolerance I already have. I quickly came to realize that book three could not be completed unless and until I finished the trailer for the film.

Without the animated scenes, I couldn't see the path book three should follow, even though I had already laid out the storyboard for it weeks before. Even the best laid plans are not the final production, and I've learned to let the imagination juices flow where the creative license allows it to go. You can see the results in book three, or in the animation via clips of scenes at PastorKeith.org/trailer.

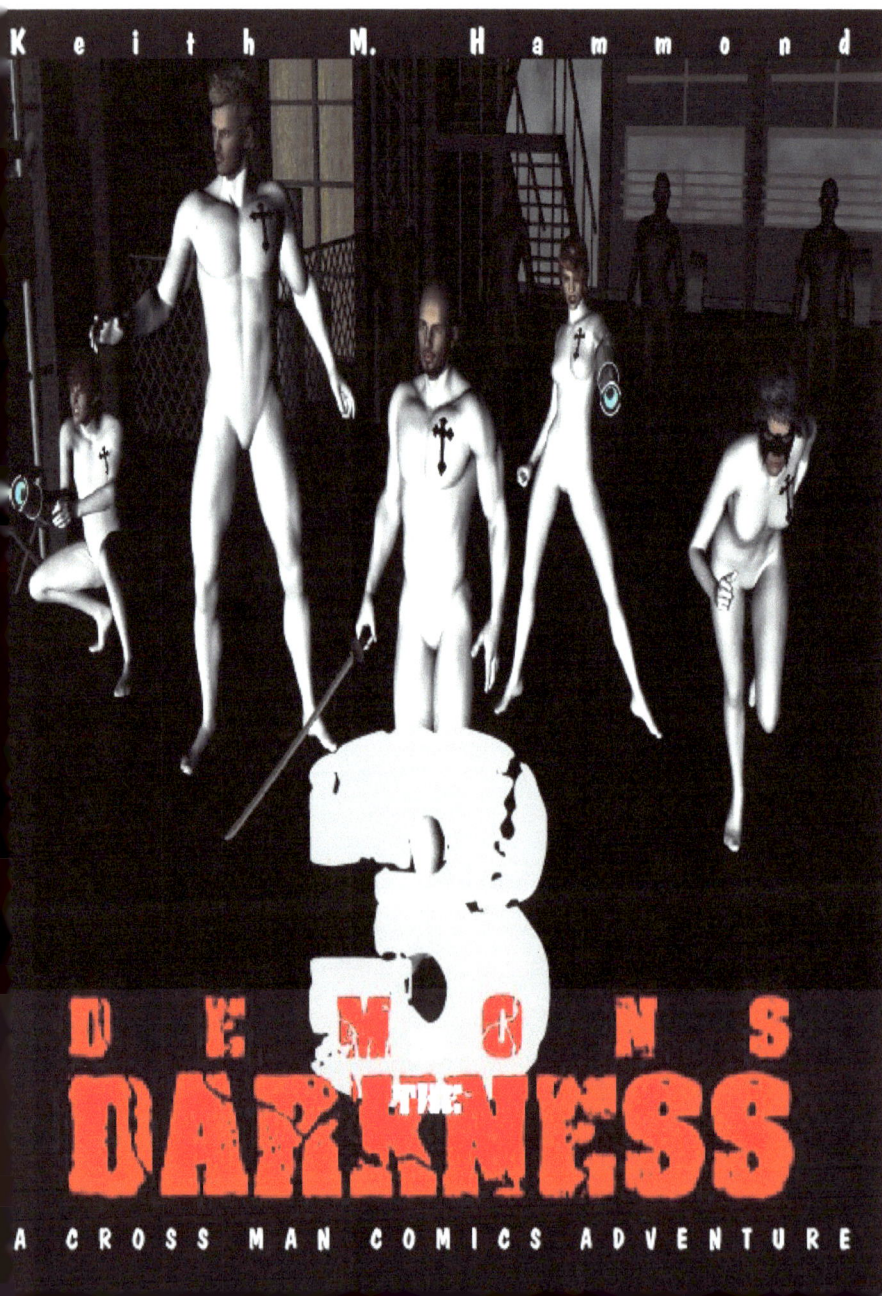

PREMISE

Book Three pushed the envelop in that it takes readers deeper into the story and beyond the boundaries of books 1 and 2.

It lets you into the script for the film and you begin to see it unfold in the story via the scenes.

Captain Cross realizes that each door he enters trying to find the Devil is just a new demon designed to distract him.

The team invades the Devil's Den only to find it empty.

The battle eventually makes it way to the actual cavern where Satan's setup is, when Rangers flying overhead notice demons coming up out of the ground.

Another amazing adventure told through the pages of this third book, which leads directly into the full story and the script.

Twists and turns leading to the trailer.

58 Pgs Paperback
ISBN 9781938588815 $12.99
Released November 2016

Available at most major retailers and at LessonsForLifeBooks.com

The Essentials

The characters of this team each have their own separate appeal and action. They come together to combine their strengths in order to defeat the Devil.

Their individual efforts are not enough alone, but as a team they are indeed a force to be reckoned with. In a battle for many boundaries normally closed that Satan is intent upon opening, they risk life and liberty to help ensure that those left behind still have hope that they too will one day make it off the planet.

Watch as CAP, STRENGTH, FOX, INTEL and SHADOW summon every ounce of faith, fight, and flight to remain fearless in this epic post-rapture battle.

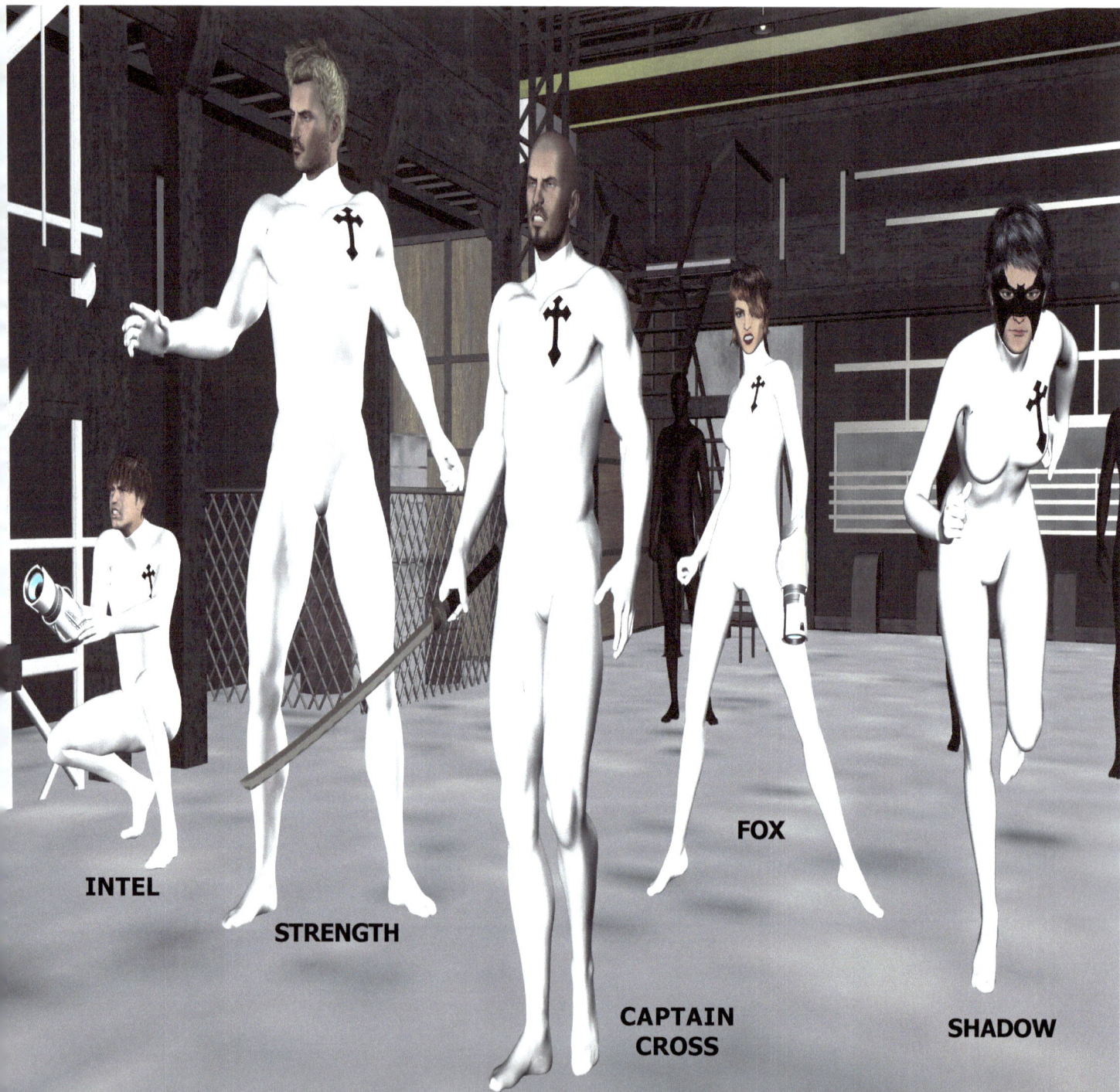

INTEL

STRENGTH

FOX

CAPTAIN
CROSS

SHADOW

Creating characters to serve as support for the core team simply flowed off the pages as the story began to develop chapter by chapter, but I also wanted them to be fully scalable into their own series at some point.

There is no magic formula for making it all work together in the same order from one project or one book to another. What happens most often for me is that I'll be asleep and I'll receive a vision or dream for one thing or another, which will flush itself out once I put it down on paper or start to bring it to life through graphics.

The characters on the support squad also have their own appeal and action. Individually, they bring great skills to the battle, and as a team, they are a force to be reckoned with.

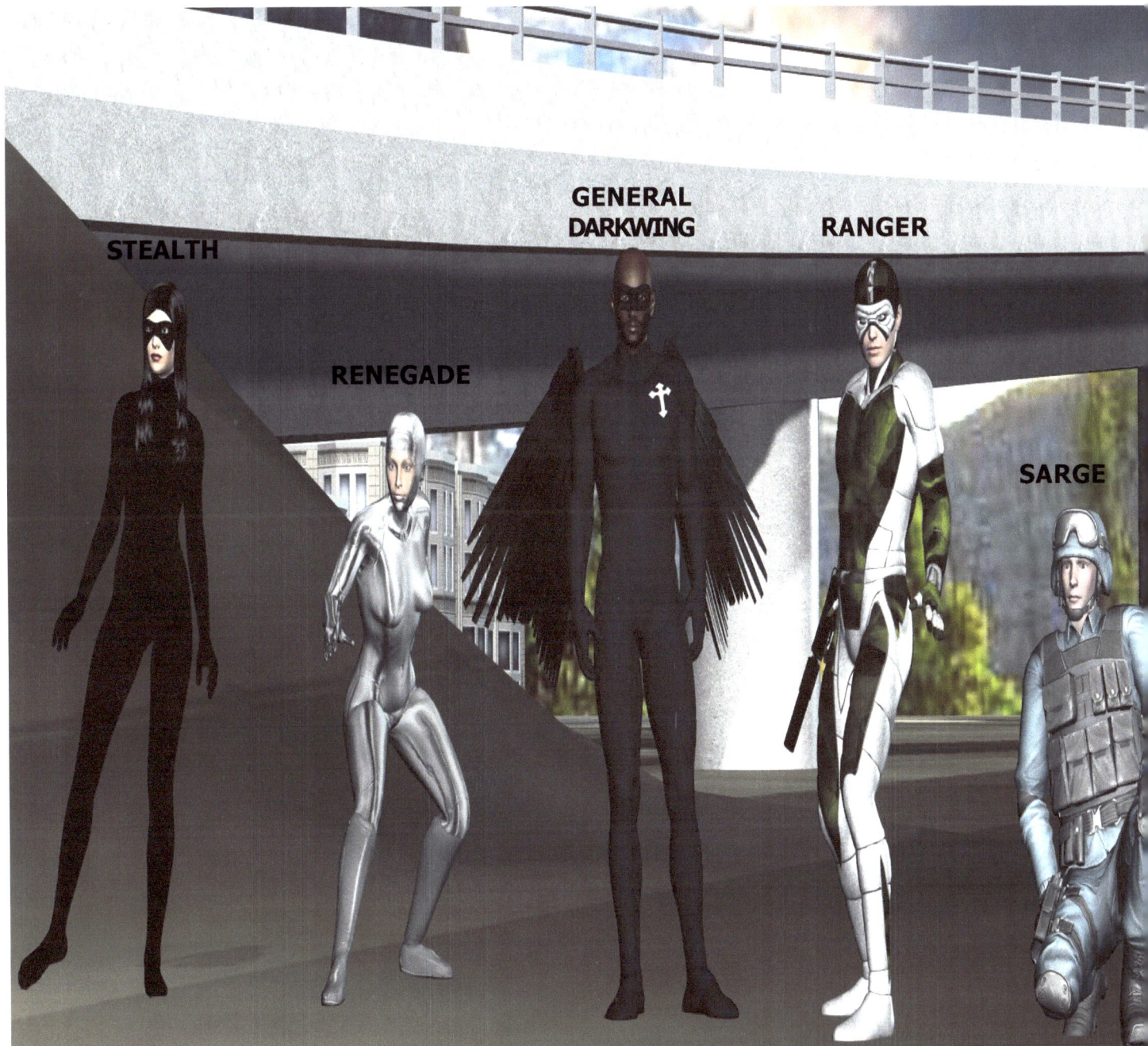

STEALTH

RENEGADE

GENERAL DARKWING

RANGER

SARGE

General Darkwing is basically me in a mask. In the beginning, my plan was to build the core team around him, but that idea didn't flow well on the pages or in the graphics. Ranger, has been his sidekick in many battles.

I passed the core lead role over to Captain Cross, and wrote the stories as I originally intended, which is for 'Cross Man' to be the star. It began to work so well this way, that I was actually surprised when I found a way to include General Darkwing in the story in book three and the film.

You just really never know how each book or each story or even each page is going to flow until you begin writing it. If the story is worth reading, I've learned that it will write itself.

Simplicity is what I've found works best when choosing actors or creating avatars to play a role. Depending on the part, the complexity of the script and the flow of the dialog some characters may not work.

I chose twins for the roles of MICRO and CIRCUIT because it gives me the most flexibility in working with the same avatar to play both parts. When Micro is managing his duties in OPS, his brother Circuit can be out in the field gathering data to help support a mission or solve a problem.

Twins have this uncanny ability to communicate with each other without speaking so I've built in the bonus of having them be able to talk telepathically.

The team's headquarters is OPS. A warehouse environment that meets the needs on many levels. It has a catwalk, grated floors, opening doors, plenty of columns and other spaces, plus a lower level accessible by stairs that fits the needs of the team quite well.

There are many facets of OPS that you'll see throughout the various books and certainly in the trailer and film, but the primary goal was to integrate a space that looks operational, but still provides for both form and function.

I think this meets the objective nicely.

15 Lab

What an amazing thing our mind is to have the capacity to help us model what we have only imagined. I'm a long time advocate of 3D animation and the incredible visions it allows us to bring to life for others to see. I've been drawing in 3D since my early childhood, using simply a pencil and ruler to do it.

Today, computers and graphics cards have replaced the work my hands used to do and does so in much less time and with far more clarity and creativity. I enjoy being able to render things that I've created and to see and utilize models that others have made.

Underneath OPS, is a lab that provides additional support to the team.

You can see both OPS and the LAB in full 3D animation by visiting PastorKeith.org/trailer

Rangers

16

Providing the team with immediate and ongoing operational support is the task of the Rangers. Using state of the art weapons and technological gadgets, they are able to surround the team with the type of ground cover needed including taking on special missions.

Whether its flanking so a team member can take flight, or laying down suppressive fire that keeps the opposition from advancing on a trapped team member, Rangers provide a plethora of support both on the ground and in the air.

See video clips of the Rangers in action at PastorKeith.org/trailer

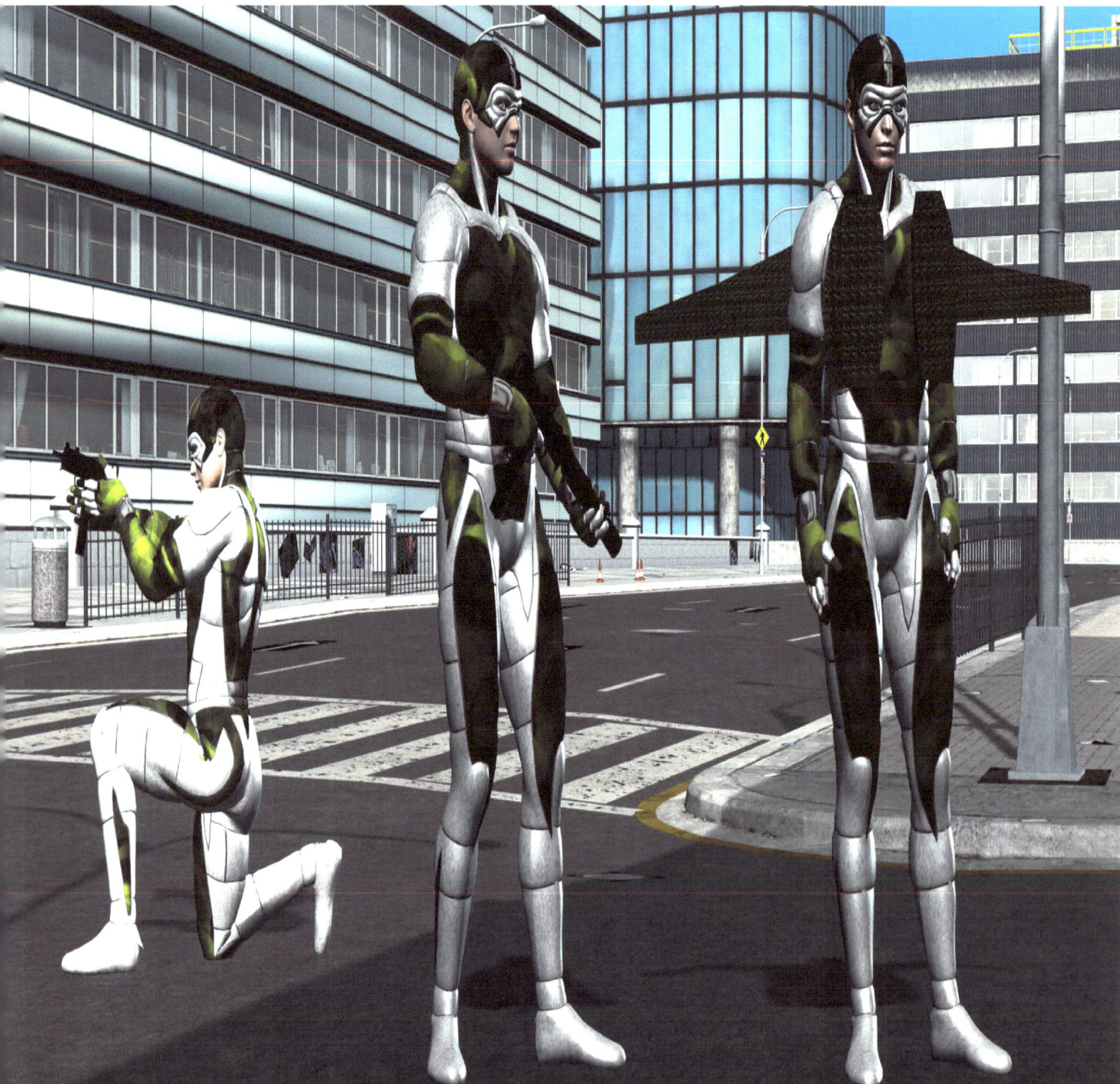

Most people may think that the job of a soldier is to fight the battle, not in this comic book series. These soldiers spend much of their time as the first line of defense in any war, but also devote themselves to finding and eliminating threats before they become dangerous to the team and the people they protect.

Soldiers scour the landscape in and outside the city for potential dangers, and when they aren't removing such issues and problems they devote themselves to training missions that help keep them prepared for any and everything that could come their way.

Soldiers spend time on offense, so they won't have to always be on the defense.

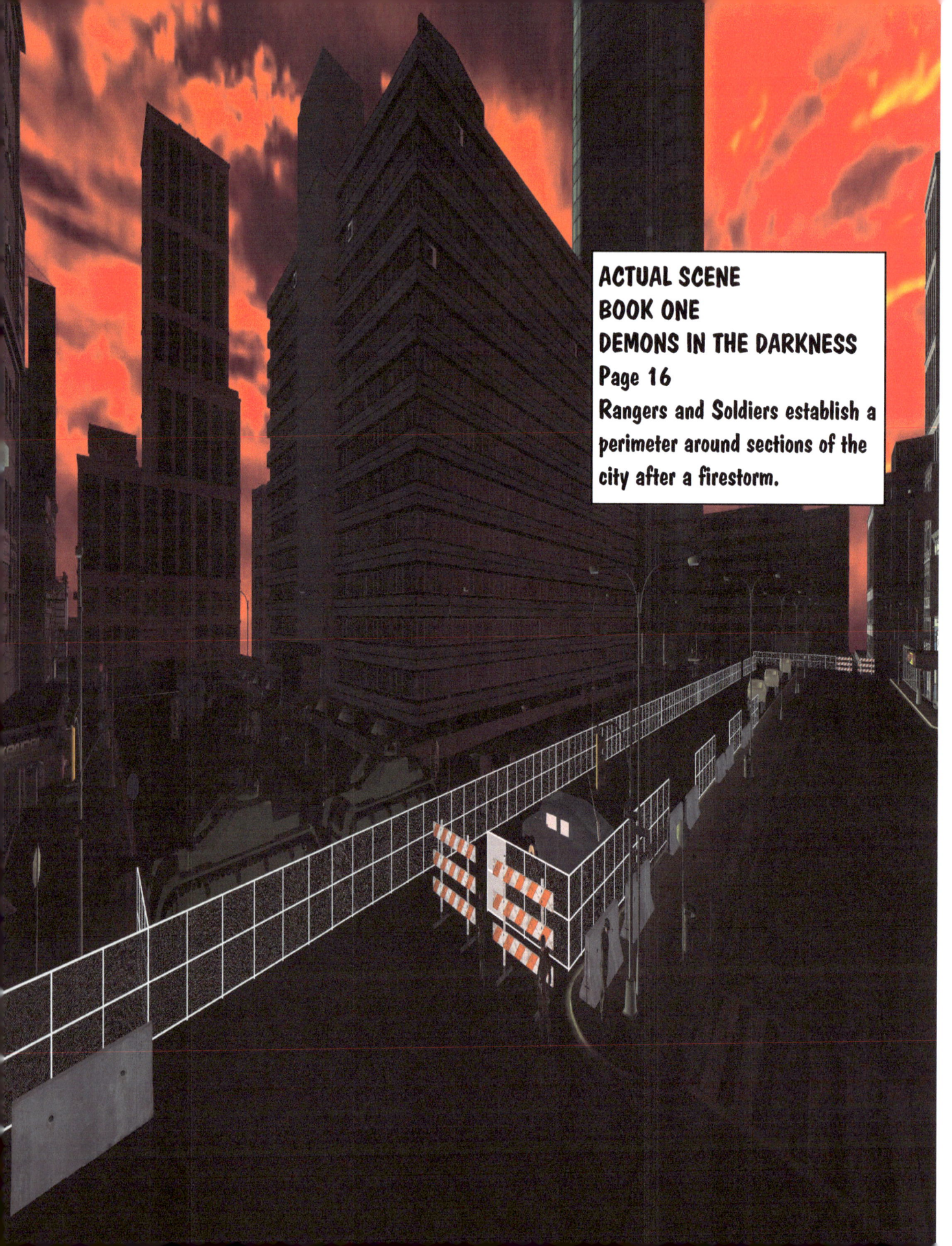

ACTUAL SCENE
BOOK ONE
DEMONS IN THE DARKNESS
Page 16
Rangers and Soldiers establish a perimeter around sections of the city after a firestorm.

The Elite

CAPTAIN CROSS

NAME: Captain Cross
ALIASES: Cross Man

RANK: Leads the Cross Team
SECRET: Com unit and supersuit

STRENGTHS: Endures extreme temps
BONUS: Can deploy wings at will

WEAPONS: Katana and Electro Blade
WATCH CLIPS: PastorKeith.org/trailer

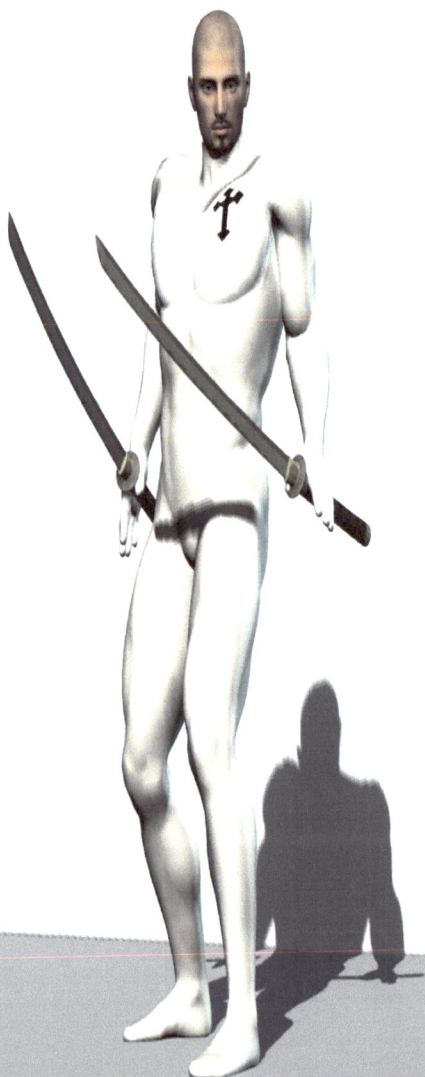

NAME: Strength
ALIASES: Power

LIKES: An avid hunter
SECRET: Com unit and supersuit

STRENGTHS: Telekinetics
BONUS: Can grow bigger and taller

WEAPONS: His hands. Can move anything.
WATCH CLIPS: PastorKeith.org/trailer

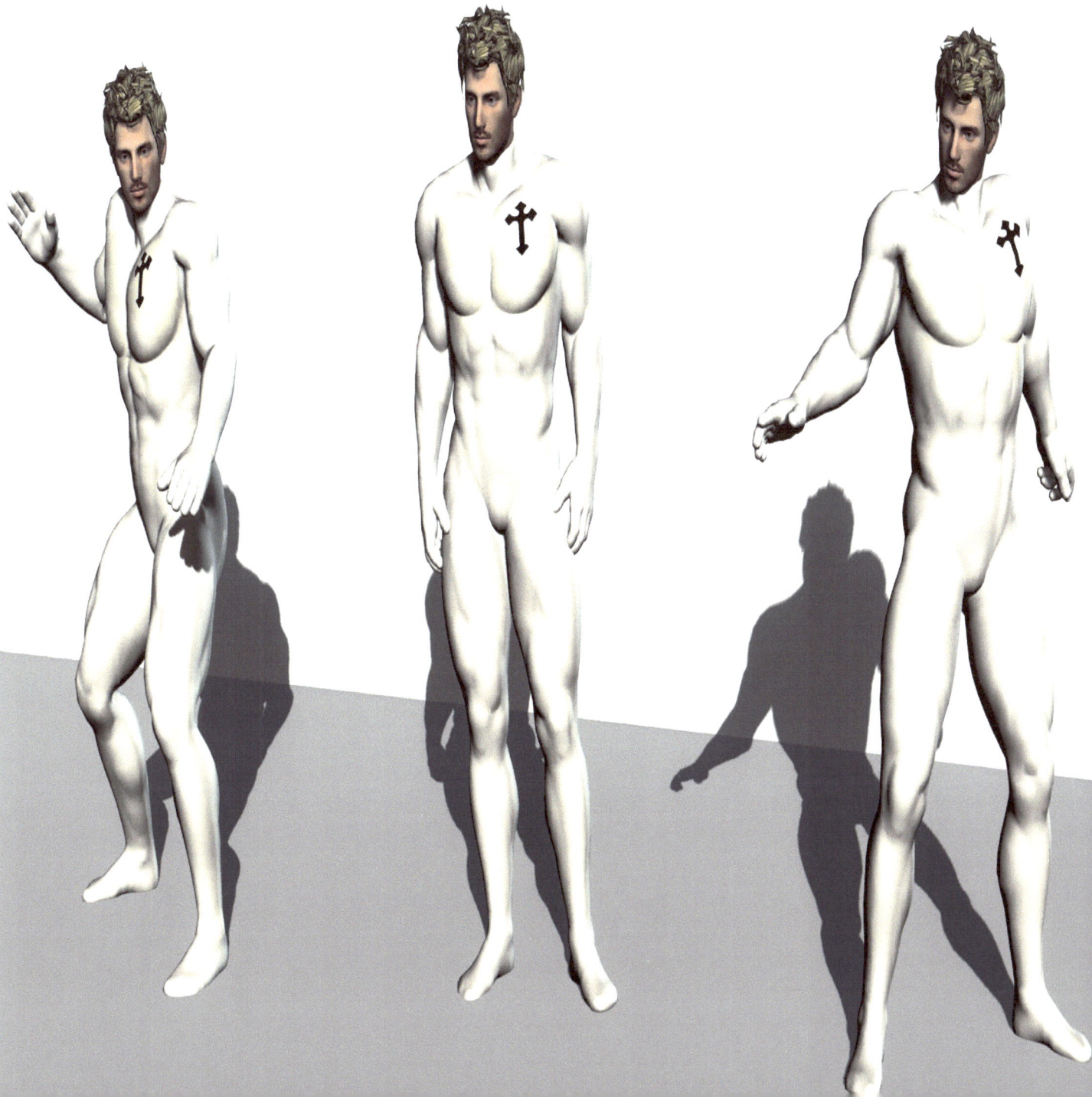

NAME:	Intel	**STRENGTHS:**	Abnormal Flexibility
ALIASES:	Memory Man	**BONUS:**	Telegraphic memory
LIKES:	Anything intellectual	**WEAPONS:**	Arm Cannon and Hover Cycle
SECRET:	Com unit and supersuit	**WATCH CLIPS:**	PastorKeith.org/trailer

NAME:	Fox	**STRENGTHS:**	Sensory Perception
ALIASES:	Sly	**BONUS:**	Human Lie Detector
LIKES:	The finer things in life	**WEAPONS:**	Arm Cannon and Hover Cycle
SECRET:	Com unit and supersuit	**WATCH CLIPS:**	PastorKeith.org/trailer

NAME: Shadow
ALIASES: Lady Flash

LIKES: Anything organic
SECRET: Scientist in the Lab at OPS

STRENGTHS: Super speed running or flying
BONUS: Can become invisible

WEAPONS: Can duplicate any shadow
WATCH CLIPS: PastorKeith.org/trailer

THE ENEMY

Devil

NAME: Satan
ALIASES: Too many to list

PLAN: World domination
SECRET: Is weakened by truth

OTHER: Serpent that lives in and around fire and hot temps.

STRENGTHS: Mind control
BONUS: Can morph into a super snake.

WEAPONS: Temptation & Suggestion
WATCH CLIPS: PastorKeith.org/trailer

NAME: Demons
ALIASES: Darkmen

PLAN: To live again as humans
SECRET: Can't live in sunlight long

OTHER: Can't think for themselves without having a leader.

STRENGTHS: Doesn't feel fear or pain
BONUS: Can endure super hot temps

WEAPONS: Overtake & morphs humans
WATCH CLIPS: PastorKeith.org/trailer

NAME:	Dragon	**STRENGTHS:**	Abnormal Agility for its size
ALIASES:	Dungeon Dweller	**BONUS:**	Can fly and use its tail to steer
PURPOSE:	Destroy humans	**WEAPONS:**	Claws, breaths fire, fangs
WEAKNESS:	The vein under its chin	**WATCH CLIPS:**	PastorKeith.org/trailer
OTHER:	Reptile that can survive in most conditions.		

NAME: Demon Dog
ALIASES: Two-headed dog

PURPOSE: Protects the Dark Lair
WEAKNESS: Fights itself if angry enough

OTHER: Adapts to its conditions.

STRENGTHS: Abnormal Agility
BONUS: Uses spiked tail as a weapon

WEAPONS: Claws, fangs, two heads
WATCH CLIPS: PastorKeith.org/trailer

Dark Lair

Satan's earthly realm is much different than his home in Hell. He takes over old abandoned cathedrals and churches to turn them into dens of sin. Dark Lair has a deep dungeon underneath that is home to most of the creatures that are under the Devil's control.

There are secret rooms and passageways and tunnels inside and underneath the Lair that lead to other parts of the city, which is how Satan always seems to get away when he is facing danger.

The fact that he can morph into a super snake or use humans as shields are simply other advantages to him being able to avoid capture.

Underneath the Dark Lair is where the depths of the dungeon are. It contains all sorts of doors that lead nowhere but around in circles, and only one of the doors leads to the Den of Sin. Difficult to find because it always randomly rotates and only lines up with the actual passage once every sixty minutes.

The dungeon is always hot and the fires are always blazing. There is a lava lake called the lake of fire under it where nothing can survive.

There is a cavern in book three and in the trailer that lead down to the dungeon but it is too dangerous for humans to enter but there are always demons, dragons and dogs coming out.

The Dark Lair is where Satan has set up shop. He has mutated certain creatures to serve as weapons against humans and the Cross Team. The Demonics have a variety of powers and abilities that can cause harm and they live in the most extreme of conditions underneath the Earth.

They cannot come to the surface, because they cannot survive in sunlight. They all have weaknesses, but the two most powerful and dangerous are Slither and Sin.

None of these creatures have ever been out or could survive outside of the darkness of the dungeons underneath the Dark Lair.

DRAGON STATUES

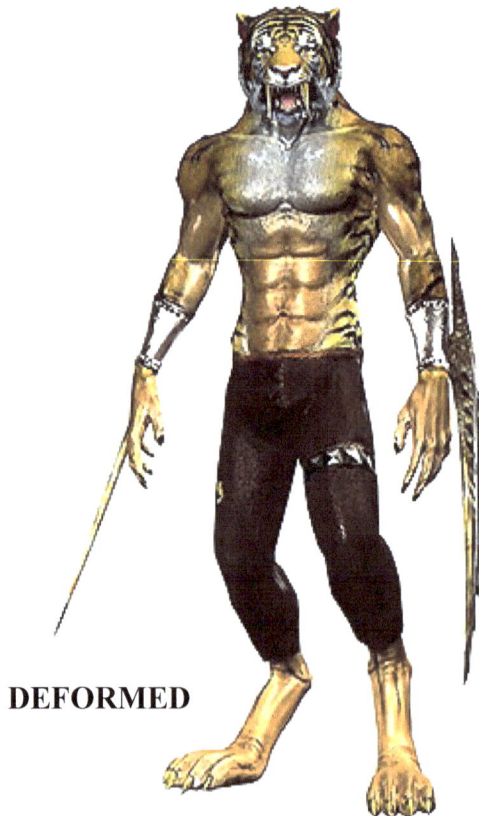

DEFORMED

DREADED

THE EXTRAS

Eliminate, eradicate and evict anything that is of the Devil from the Earth. The mission is clear and concise and the entire Cross Team, plus those who provide support are committed to the cause.

The mission for me as the man entrusted with this incredible initiative is to continue to share this story and all that comes out of it, through the methods and mediums such as books, films, and gaming.

I look forward to the endeavor of experiencing the enormous benefit of being able to brand this historic story in a new and different way. The events contained with the context of the story are paraphrased, thus the manner in which they are conveyed to the various audiences is vastly different for that very reason.

Cross Man Comics is committed to taking this series to the next level. We are in the process of working on programming a game based on the books and the film.

Demons in the Darkness is gaining ground and those who see the characters, and read the books all have the same or similar reaction. This lets us know that we're on to something.

I never saw the books or the series coming but when the storyboards and layout began to take shape on the screen in the form of graphics and avatars, books, trailer and film, I knew the next level would lead into gaming. Enjoy the scenes and screenshots from the books, trailer and film.

A man working inside a food warehouse being chased by a demon.

Rangers taking down a stronghold of the Devil and his demons.

After a city wide evacuation, these people decided to stay behind.

FOX and INTEL engaged in a very meaningful conversation.

Rangers blown back when a church they are checking out explodes.

44

SHADOW using her speed to run across the top of the water.

STRENGTH using his mind to lift and throw demons attacking him.

46

Team members in plain clothes discussing who is going to corral a two-headed dog.

People running from demons find themselves trapped.

GENERAL DARKWING explains to **CAP** how he became a General.

SHADOW saving kids from the cancer ward of a burning hospital.

52

KEEP
CLEAR

A couple gets attacked from behind suddenly by a group of demons.

The Devil and his demons holding **INTEL** hostage at the cavern.

More About the Author...

Book signings are an incredible way that readers, fans and followers can spend time with an author, and to ask questions. Keith M. Hammond is available to meet with small or large groups anywhere in the USA and possibly in other parts of the world. Send your invite or request via the link below.

+ Send Invites and Requests via

PastorKeith.org/contact

As an author, I'm always appreciative of anyone who takes time out of their day to reach out to me with input or inspiration for anything I'm working on. I've been entrusted with an incredibly innovative way of giving people hope through the books I write, and this new visual way of helping people to see the battles many of us face each and every day is amazing.

Thank you for your support and I look forward to hearing from you at anytime.

www.ingramcontent.com/pod-product-compliance
Lightning Source LLC
LaVergne TN
LVHW072107070426

835509LV00002B/48